T0131456

My Heart Longs for the Lord

Draw Near to God and He Will Draw Near to You

Lei Cantrell

authorHOUSE®

AuthorHouse™
1663 Liberty Drive
Bloomington, IN 47403
www.authorhouse.com
Phone: 1 (800) 839-8640

Published by AuthorHouse 07/17/2018

ISBN: 978-1-5462-5093-7 (sc)
ISBN: 978-1-5462-5092-0 (e)

Print information available on the last page.

Contents

Acknowledgment

I would like to give thanks and honor to our Father in Heaven. My life has never been the same since He asked me to "Seek Him," in a vision twenty-five years ago. Christ said: **"I am the Way, the Truth and the Life"** (John 14:6). By daily walking with our Lord, I experience more and more of Him. He has become my Way, my Truth, and my Life. I could not have come this far without the Saving Grace of our God.

My special thanks to Southern Heights Bible Church – my church family. Thank you for your prayers and encouragement. Thank you Pastor Charles Nickel for teaching me patience. I appreciate you very much.

To my husband: I love how you edit this book for me. Thank you, darling.

For my children: To see them grow in the Lord has truly blessed my heart. I praise God they are such wonderful gifts.

To Stewart Overbey: I thank you for your inspiration. I pray for you, your wife Jodi, and your ministry to continue to grow.

To my general manager Gary Arturo at Ryans Restaurant: I appreciate your wonderful leadership and training.

To my current management and co-workers at Chick-Fil-A: I thank you for your prayers and support. Thanks especially for Mr. Brian and Ms. Robbin for their inspiration in leading by example, I thank God for you.

To Mr. Marcus, the general manager at the Dollar Tree store: It is my great honor to work for you, and I appreciate you for tolerating me. I praise the Lord for using you to inspire me. Also thank my co-worker Connie and assistant manager Carla at the Dollar Tree store, who encourage and pray for me along the way. May God Bless you!

Father, I thank you for everything you have done for me: For patiently walking with me; For leading me; For the marvelous wonders you have been showing me; For all of my friends who have enriched my life! Lord, I pray for you to bless them. I pray for this book to be a blessing to others who are seeking and longing for you. As I am dedicating the book, "My Heart Longs For The LORD" to our Heavenly Father: May God be glorified. With my grateful heart, I praise and worship you. In Jesus' name, Amen!

Introduction

"God is Love." He often reveals Himself in special ways to show His Love to us.

A friend once said that this life is a big classroom. God has us in the classroom to learn the lessons. He is the Teacher and uses the obstacles as the means for us to learn of His love, His discipline, of His Sovereignty. Through learning, we draw closer to God. He reveals more of Himself to us as we grow more mature and become more intimate with Him. **"As ye have therefore received Christ Jesus the Lord, so walk ye in him: Rooted and built up in him, and stablished in the faith, as ye have been taught, abounding therein with thanksgiving"** (Colossians 2:6,7).

Even though it has never been easy, God has always been faithful. He has always been there to strengthen me with His Love, guiding me with His Holy Spirit. I am thankful for what He has done. **"O Come, let us sing unto the LORD: let us make a joyful noise to the rock of our salvation. Let us come before His presence with thanksgiving, and make a joyful noise unto him with Psalms"** (Psalm 95:1,2).

As I am dedicating "My Heart Longs For The Lord" to our Father in Heaven, I would like to invite you on a journey to see how He has been revealing Himself through the obstacles of this life to cause me to grow in Him. May we glorify His Holy Name through this book, in Jesus' name, Amen!

Foreword

by Tim Cantrell

Several years ago, my wife woke me up early one morning saying, "I have a song from the LORD: She sang, "My heart longs for the LORD." Immediately, I got up and went out for a walk. Following is the recorded result:

My Heart Longs for The LORD

My Heart Longs for The LORD
His Glory and His Grace
To know His sweet Will
To see His smiling Face
My heart longs for the LORD
To keep His Word
to be Filled with His Spirit
and be Armed with His Sword

My Heart longs for the LORD
to Know His Truth
Jesus sets me free
to Overcome this world
My heart longs for the LORD

to Trust in Him
to Give Him all the Glory
and to Praise His Name

This world is passing away
and all the lusts thereof
O LORD, SAVE ME, I pray
no more going astray
I long to keep my mind
always on Things Above
to be Filled with His Spirit
and be Armed with His Love

My Lord was Crucified
It was for me He Died
It is no more I who live
in Him I will Abide
I long to Keep His Word
unto the very end
to be Filled with His Spirit
and be Washed in His Blood

My Lord is Reigning Above
He is Alive and well
He is Coming Again
Now let us Go and Tell
You must be "Born Again"
You must be Ready Now

Let us Serve Him Today
Let us "Watch and Pray"

I long to Preach His Word
and let the Truth be known
to set others Free
to Make His Glory Shown
He is The Way, The Truth
The Only Way to Life
and I'm longing to Live
with Him Eternally

By Him, the Work is Done
and the Race is run
His Word is fulfilled
Our Wills must be One
I long to Overcome
to know the Vict'ry's won
and I'm longing to hear
from Him, "My child, well done."

It is not enough to sing about it – IT MUST BE LIVED! It is my prayer that you will be Blessed through the simplicity of the profound Truth contained in this book.

Thursday, October 28, 2004   12:46:56 PM

Written By Lei Cantrell

Chapter One

The Struggle and God's Sovereignty

I am writing this testimony to encourage God's people that God is in control of your lives. Sometimes when the situation which you are facing makes you feel like you can't get out of the bottom of the pit, I want to remind you that He is with you no matter where you are. He is a Merciful and Loving God, and we should look up to Him for comfort and refuge.

I was pregnant again and found out it was a boy. By the third trimester, my doctor told me that I had gestational diabetes, and this time the doctors put me on insulin to keep the blood sugar low.

Compared with my first pregnancy, my husband and I were facing a more difficult situation. This time our bills are piled upon bills. And the most frustrating thing was that we don't have insurance or medicaid, because my husband is so bullheaded that he would not use any of these for help. I was completely stressed out. When I found out that I had to be put on insulin, I was devastated – that meant more bills to pay.

I was rather annoyed with my six-year-old daughter who was trying to comfort me by telling me everything is going to be all right. I was mad at my husband, and as matter of fact, I felt like I was mad at everybody and everything. My husband told me to pray, but I didn't want to listen.

I don't know how long it took me to calm down, until I sat down one morning by myself. I cried out to the Lord, and asked for His forgivness for my bad temper. I prayed that He would help me to be calm and treat everybody nicely. I asked the Lord to help us financially. As soon as I prayed, I heard the voice of the Lord as clear as a bell, which is still ringing in my ear, "Do not be afraid, for I AM with you, and I am suffering with you. So do it gladly unto the Lord." The most wonderful peace flowed into my heart and soul, and His joy returned to me. However, the following weeks did not go smoother. My husband had planned to make more money by running the route to Arkansas for four days a week, but that didn't turn out to be God's plan. And then the station wagon died on us. Normally when these kind of things happen, I would be panicking and depressed. But this time, the peace of the Lord continued. The best way to describe the continued overflowing peace would be like the Lord has used a lock and locked the peace in me and threw away the key. Just like the scripture where it is written: **"O that thou hadst hearkened to my commandments! then had thy peace been as a river, and thy righteousness as the waves of the sea"** (Isaiah 48:18). And Jesus has said in the Gospel of John, **"Peace I leave with you, my peace I give unto you:**

not as the world giveth, give I unto you. Let not your heart be troubled, neither let it be afraid" (John 14:27).

How many times have we struggled with the difficulties in our daily lives, and have forgotten to look up to the Lord and ask for guidance and assurance. Through this testimony, I see myself as Peter in Matthew 14:25-32. When Peter saw Jesus walking on the water, he wanted to go to Jesus. When Peter was walking towards Jesus on the water, he saw the wind was boisterous, he was afraid and began to sink. So he cried out, "Lord, save me." Jesus stretched out His hand immediately and caught him, and said unto him, "O thou of little faith, wherefore didst thou doubt?"

Don't we all act like Peter sometimes? We all want to be like Jesus, and we all want to go to Him. But when we start facing the struggles, and lose our focus on the Lord, we forget that He is Sovereign! We must remember as we keep our focus on Him, that He is able to deliver us through all things.

Through a C-section, our son Josiah Dwight Cantrell was born on Friday, October 15th, at 4:28 pm. We praise the Lord for the blessing He has given. Blessed be the name of the Lord. I would like to close with the message of a song, "The Anchor Holds." Susanne, from our church, sings this song occasionally on Sunday mornings. I think it fits here perfectly. It says when we go through the storms, the Lord is there, and He is our Anchor.

I thank the Lord for His Sovereignty. Focus on Him, we shall be in good shape. Praise the Name of the LORD, Amen!

Sunday, December 11, 2005   12:35:14 PM

Written by Lei Cantrell

Chapter Two

Are You Prepared?

At the time of this writing (December 2005), it has been over a year since Old Country Buffet closed. I have been wanting to express how I feel for so long, and now I think it is time. The Lord has inspired me to write about my experience. I would like to share my feelings with all believers. First, I want to thank the Lord for the opportunities to serve Him. I pray for the new year, that the Lord will give clear direction and understanding of what is happening and how we should follow His Will, according to His Purpose and timing.

My world turned upside down with a simple phone call from work at 3 pm, Sunday, November 28th. The manager told my husband, "Old Country Buffet is closed." Our son, Josiah Dwight Cantrell was born Friday, October 15th. I went back to work on Thanksgiving Day. I had several costomers come up and ask me, "I heard you are going to close. Is that true?" My answer to them was, "I doubt it."

Even though I had heard about it so many times, I never believed it. I was shocked, depressed, and extremely angry.

I felt lost. Old Country Buffet had been like a mission field for me, and now, suddenly, with a simple call, it was over.

I prayed and prayed, and realized that my mission at OCB was complete, and that the Lord will assign a new mission for me. Besides, I do have an important job to do – to take care of my son. He is such a joy. And now he is over a year old, very active, crawling, and getting into things. While caring for my son and waiting, the Word of the Lord reminded me of a parable Jesus gave in Matthew 25, the parable of "The Ten Virgins."

The ten virgins took their lamps and were getting ready to meet the bridegroom. Five of them were wise, and five of them were foolish. The wise filled their lamps with oil, the foolish ones did not. While the bridegroom tarried, they all went to sleep. At midnight, the cry rang out, "The bridegroom is coming," and they all went out to meet him. The foolish ones' lamps burned out, so while they went to buy the oil, the Lord came and took the wise (ready) ones in, but the foolish ones were shut out.

What does the Oil in this parable represent? It represents the Holy Spirit who dwells in us. One may ask why is it important to have the Holy Spirit? Allow me to explain it in a simple way. When we read certain verses in the scripture, and don't understand them, we pray for understanding. The Spirit of the Lord serves as an instructor in our being, to help us see the meaning in our mind and heart. It is an "eye-opener" in a spiritual sense. When we seek guidance in making decisions, the Holy Spirit serves as a counselor, to guide and direct us in line with the Will of God according to His Word in that area. When we are in turmoil, whether physical or emotional, the Holy Spirit serves as our comforter.

I would like to share the following characteristics of the Holy Spirit, so that we may have a better understanding of Him:

1. The Holy Spirit has and gives us knowledge of God (1 Corinthians 2:10,11).
2. The Holy Spirit has Will – He makes determinations (1 Corinthians 12:11).
3. The Holy Spirit has a mind and prays (Romans 8:27).
4. The "fruit of the Spirit is love" (Galatians 5:22).
5. The Holy Spirit is able to grieve (Ephesians 4:30).
6. The Holy Spirit is Wisdom. (Isaiah 11:2).
7. The Holy Spirit Teaches and Speaks. (John 14:26), (Nehemiah 9:20), (Hebrews 3:7-9), (Revelation 2:7).

These are some of the characteristics of the Holy Spirit. I trust they not only have opened our eyes and minds to see Him, and to better understand our experience with God through His Spirit, but it also helps us to better understand Jesus' parable.

The Lord has spoken, **"Watch therefore, for ye know neither the day nor the hour wherein the Son of man cometh"** (Matthew 25:13).

From this scripture, I would like to remind all of us, that we should be like the wise virgins who filled their lamps will oil – that is with the Holy Spirit, who actively dwells in us (John 14:17). So that, when Jesus comes, He will take us into the marriage fully prepared. But as for those foolish ones, without the Holy Spirit dwelling in them, they were shut out.

So, my question for you is: "Are you prepared?"

Chapter Three

"Love Your Neighbor As Yourself"
(Matthew 22:39 NIV)

In a conversation, the subject of Jesus' example of washing his disciple's feet was discussed. How could the Son of God wash their feet, and should we as His followers wash each other's feet also?

Let's look at John 13:8. When Peter refused to let Jesus wash his feet, Jesus answered: "If I wash thee not, thou hast no part with me." Christ washing the disciples' feet symbolized God's cleansing of our sin, and receiving us. Jesus was setting an example of humility, as he washed us clean with a servant's heart, in order to show us how to share His love with others, and to humble ourselves before God and man. We should follow Christ's example to serve one another. I can sense someone thinking, "It is true Christ used this as an example in his time, and we practice that at church. But how do we show his humility to the world?" Let me share an example.

In July 2004, we moved into a house in a quiet neighborhood. The Knapps were our next door neighbors.

Over the years, we became good friends. Mrs. Knapp taught me to crochet. As a nurse, Janice has always come to the rescue when I needed advice on which kind of medicine to give to the kids when they were sick. And she helped me with taking the kids to school in bad weather. Ricky Knapp has always been so helpful to my husband with car troubles, and other things needing repair. The list can go on and on.

I have often interpreted the verse – "Love your neighbor as yourself –" that we should be friendly, caring, and have peace with our neighbors. However, the ice storm of January 2007 raised my understanding of that Scripture to a higher level.

The ice storm hit the whole area. I had never seen anything like this before. The situation sent city utility workers running crazy to restore power – they were so short on staff. Most households had to wait for days, even weeks in some spots. The trees were frozen with trunks cracked open as if someone had chopped it with a giant axe. Many branches broke off from the ice being so heavy. Businesses and schools were closed due to the severe weather and horrible road conditions.

In our case, several large branches broke off and fell on the power line, pulling it all the way to the ground and thus bending the weather head. As a result, part of our house had power (110), and part didn't (no 220). This meant we couldn't use the oven or stove to cook. We couldn't take a hot shower. We had no heat in the house. I felt like an Eskimo in an igloo. Our fridge became regular food storage. The garage however became a fridge where it was so cold that we could put dairy and meat out there.

In the midst of the chaos, the love of God came through. The Knapps used a generator. They allowed us to run a long extension cord from their house, so that we could have heat, take a hot shower, and warm our food in the microwave. That lasted for almost three weeks. I really have no words to describe my gratitude to them.

It is through the storms of life our faith in Christ is tested. The ice storm not only tested my faith, but it also revealed the true meaning of how Christ has commanded us to act in love.

I could not be more proud to have such wonderful neighbors – a special blessing from God that I will treasure forever. I praise God for them. I give thanks and honor for them as the Light and Love of God shines through. Thank you Lord for teaching me this lesson through the storm. Amen!

Sunday, June 26, 2005   5:47:42 PM

Written by Lei Cantrell

Chapter Four

When I was "Naked, Ye Clothed Me"
(Matthew 25:36)

From The parable of the talents (Matthew 25:14-30), we understand that everyone of us has God-given talents. It is in obedience to our Lord, that we go forward to share the good news in a variety of ways to describe the wonders and knowledge of our God. By using the God-given talent wisely, God will reward us. But for those who misuse or ignore God's gift, it is certainly displeasing to the Lord.

I learned to sew from the ladies of our church. It has been a great experience. But sewing is easier said than done for me. When the ladies were teaching me how to sew, I thought I would never get it, as slow a learner as I am. I greatly admire the beautiful dresses and cute shirts and pants, which Burnice and Shirley made. They can sit there talking and laughing and sewing at the same time, and don't make mistakes often, and then an hour later – Wa La! the outfit is finished, looking as easy as a feather. They are sewing for the school-age kids who can't afford new clothes, and it is a ministry.

I decided to join these ladies' Wednesday morning sewing club. I got so nervous when I was just cutting out the patterns, and don't even mention reading the instructions – they were like a foreign language to me. It took me a month to finish my first jumper with Burnice's help, step by step.

Personally, I didn't plan to bother sewing any more, because it was so hard for me. But that wasn't God's plan. Shirley passed on the compliment from the lady who picked up the clothes: When she saw my jumper, and she liked it very much. That encouragement did its job. I decided to try again. And after much practice, and many mistakes, it finally clicked – I had learned to sew.

After a year, I enjoy it very much. It is not that I don't make mistakes anymore, I still get frustrated to a certain degree. When this happens, Burnice, Shirley and Emma encourage me to "Take a deep breath, get up from there, and go do something else. Then come back to it later." That advice has worked pretty well.

I don't think I will ever be able to sew as perfect as other ladies, but I remember what Christ has said, **"For I was hungered, you gave me meat . . . Naked, and ye clothed me . . . ye have done it unto me"** (Matthew 25: 35, 36, 40). I agree with Burnice that we may not cloth all of them, but the Lord knows that we have done it for His sake.

Let us thank the Lord for giving us the opportunities to share about Him. May the Holy Spirit guide us in seeking our Father in Heaven, and to stand firm with Him. So Lord, I pray that you will help us to do what you commanded us to do, to "Love one another," and to have compassion on each other. And I pray that you will continue to bless the sewing ministry, in Jesus name, Amen! **"Come, ye blessed of my Father, inherit the Kingdom prepared for you from the foundation of the world"** (Matthew 25:34).

Tuesday, December 20, 2005   04:24:10 PM

Written By Lei Cantrell

Chapter Five

A Miracle of God

The purpose of this testimony is for everyone to see that sometimes our Lord works miracles in people's lives. As the birthday of our Lord approaches, I want to remind everyone, that He is the Miracle above all miracles. So, let us glorify Him in this special time.

According to the four Gospels, we marvel how Jesus fed five thousand people with five loaves of bread and two fishes. (Matthew 14:13-21), (Mark 6:30-44), (Luke 9:10-17), (John 6:1-14). But to the people of modern days, not everyone can see or rather believe that Jesus still performs miracles. Well, the story which I am going to tell should prove to everyone that He is the Mighty One who does the miracle. He still provides and is the Miracle of all Himself.

The story goes back to a Friday morning, at the end of August, a week before school started. I was reading an e-mail from Frank and Tami Phillips, a missionary couple to Utah. Tami wrote, "The Lord has blessed them in their work and they were very busy. Thankfully her sister was there to help her, and taught her to sew." When I read that, the Lord spoke to me immediately saying, "It would be a good idea to make some clothes for her children." I e-mailed Tami and asked whether she would like for us to make some clothes for her children? I suppose that she was quite surprised, but she said it would be very nice for us to do so. Then, I started to wonder where I will get materials to make the clothes?

A friend Celeste had given me some material some time ago from her mother's closet, so I decided to call to ask her if she could find some more fabric for me. The line was busy when I called the first time, and then no one was home when I called the second time. I did not leave a message, I thought I would just talk to her Sunday at church.

Saturday morning, about 8:15, while I was fixing my daughter breakfast, the door bell rang. I had no clue who would come to visit us this early. I opened the door and my jaw dropped: There was a pile of beautiful material sitting on the chair on my front porch. I looked out to see Celeste walking to her truck. She came back to me and said, "I cleaned my mother's closet yesterday, and found this material. I thought Lei may need them for sewing, so I will take them to her." She asked me, "Do you need them? If you don't, I will just throw them away."

I was so excited I was jumping up and down. I gave her a big hug. And I said to her, "Celeste, you are such a blessing. You don't know how the Lord has used you to answer my prayer." She stood there with astonishment. After I explained to her the situation, she was quite happy she brought the material on time. Thanks be to God.

Tami received the clothes we made just in time for Christmas. She told me that Katie wanted to try every one of them on in a hurry. The Lord knew the heart of His children, and He answered my silent prayer in a special way. The scripture says, **"Before they call I will answer; while they are still speaking I will hear"** (Isaiah 65:24).

Some people may say this is just coincedence. Well, I want to tell you this: God does not make things happen by luck or coincedence. He performs the miracle to show His love for us, to draw us closer to Him, to follow Him and to do His Will.

As we are preparing our hearts for the Lord's birthday, it actually makes this testimony more meaningful. Therefore, let us give thanks to our Heavenly Father, who sends Jesus to us, which is the Miracle above all miracles. Let us glorify Him for what He has done during this special time. Let us celebrate the Lord's birthday with a grateful heart. And to be reminded His name is called Emmanuel – God With Us.

"Praise waiteth for thee, O God, in Sion: and unto thee shall the vow be performed. O thou that hearest prayer" (Psalm 65:1,2).

Sunday, September 21, 2014   11:37:00 PM

Written by Lei D. Cantrell

Chapter Six

Is Your name Written Down In the Book Of Life?

My daughter Leianna is now a Junior in high school. She has occasionally asked me to sit down with her to look for colleges online. I cannot believe how fast the time has flown by, that she is now a beautiful young lady, keeping herself busy with softball games, and playing violin in the orchestra. And she has decided what she wants to do in life.

As I recall, the very first "grown-up" conversation we had was the summer of 2005, when she was 7 years old. I took her to attend Vacation Bible School at South Haven Baptist Church. I remember after the bible school was over, we had lunch at Jade East Chinese restaurant. So while we were enjoying our food, I asked her how she liked the bible school. She looked at me and said: "Mommy, I received Jesus today." I tried hard not to scream with excitement! "Tell me all about it, please," I asked. "Well, the teacher used a glass to represent us, and the glass was filled with water which represents sin. Then the teacher used a straw to represent Jesus. She puts the straw in the glass to suck the water out to show that Jesus took our sin so we could be free of sin." Then she looked at me seriously and stated: "Oh mommy, I have sinned a lot. I made you upset many times, and I am sorry."

I was quite mesmerized by her speech. "And by the way Mommy, God will take care of your job situation. I think why Old Country Buffet closed down was for you to rest well, and meanwhile to take care of Josiah." Old Country Buffet, where I had worked for 8 years was closed in November 2004. Our son Josiah was born October 15th, 2004.

At that moment, I was totally speechless. I tried hard to hold back my tears. My husband and I have prayed for her to receive Christ as her Lord and Savior ever since she was a baby. But I could not believe the Lord answered prayers in such an unusual way. As I looked at her and saw the light of God in her face, and the conversation she had with me felt like she was a grown woman. I praised the Lord, who works in such marvelous ways.

I remember we came home after lunch, I called and told everybody I could think of the exciting news, and I was crying and laughing. I was rejoicing over the wonder of what God has done.

That was 10 years ago, though its memory is still fresh. I remember the song, "There's a new name written down in Glory, And it's mine. Oh yes, it's mine!" Sure enough, there was a new name written in the Book of Life that day, and it was Leianna's. Praise the Lord!

She has since grown much spiritually. She has been active at church as well as at school.

Now my question is, do you know the Lord? Have you considered receiving Christ as your Lord and Savior? If not, why not seek Him? For He has declared: **"I love them that love me; and those that seek me early shall find me"** (Proverbs 8:17). And I am sure Heaven will rejoice when there is a new name written down in the Book of Life. Glory to God in the Highest. Amen!

Tuesday, September 11, 2007   3:18:51 PM

Written By Lei Deng Cantrell

Chapter Seven

God's Sufficient Grace And A Lesson on Submission

Whoever reads this title might be puzzled and wonder what does God's grace have to do with submission?

"God resists the proud, but gives grace unto the humble"

(1 Peter 5:5).

Please be patient, let me pray, and then I will tell you the story. Lord, as I am sharing this testimony with others, I pray that whoever reads this story will learn from this lesson, and submit themselves to you and to those you choose to set over them. And to learn that your Love for us is deep, and your Grace is sufficient. In Jesus' name, Amen!

It has been over a year since I started to work at Ryan's restaurant. As a baker, I like to have all my supplies ready, in order to avoid a panic attack. For this reason, I would get most of my supplies, and try to have the major baking done before the busy hours. It had been my habit, and had become my comfort zone until Mr. Bill started to work there six months ago.

As the assistant manager and as the head of the bakery, his appearance has turned my comfort zone up-side down. His managing method is that he likes the food to be made fresh and delicious. I understand his theory, but I couldn't adjust to his way of managing. Whenever he was working, I felt like I could never get my baking done. Mr. Bill is determined to stay with his managing method, which to me is nerve-racking.

During this six month period, My husband has tried to advise me to obey whatever Mr. Bill tells me to do. The general manager Mr. Gary and assistant manager Mr. Dell suggested that I need not be bullheaded with Mr. Bill. I disobeyed, I argued with Mr. Bill, and I determined to do whatever made me feel comfortable, without realizing that my not submitting to Mr. Bill's authority as the head of the bakery has angered the Lord. People say that "The Fall comes after Pride." In my case, the Lord was gracious – a serious meeting was awaiting me in the office. Before my general manager and Mr. Bill, I was warned to change my rebellious behavior, otherwise I would be removed from the bakery.

I can't tell you how stunned I was. Sometimes when a child of God is going astray, the Lord has to scold them to get his or her attention to turn back to him. In my case, I know I should show respect to my management, because the Word of the Lord teaches,

"Obey them that have the rule over you, and submit yourselves: for they watch for your

souls, as they that must give account, that they may do it with joy, and not with grief: for that is unprofitable for you" (Hebrew 13:17).

I thank the Lord for the lesson which I have learned. I praise the Lord for having me work under my management, especially that he uses Mr. Bill to teach me submission, even though it is hard to do. I am grateful for Mr. Gary – the general manager who showed grace to me, and gave me a chance to correct my wrong-doing. So may I honor Mr. Gary, for being patient with me, to whom the Grace of God has shown through you. I praise the Lord for you.

For the Word of the Lord has proclaimed, **"The Lord is merciful and gracious, slow to anger, and plenteous in mercy. He will not always chide: neither will he keep his anger forever"** (Psalm 103:8,9).

As for Mr. Bill, I thank the Lord for using you to teach me obedience and submission.

"Our fathers disciplined us for a little while as they thought best; but God disciplines us for our good, that we may share in his holiness. No discipline seems pleasant at the time, but painful. Later on, however, it produces a harvest of righteousness and peace for those have been trained by it"

(Hebrews 12:10,11 NIV).

Tuesday, August 25, 2009   03:48:46 AM

Written by Lei D. Cantrell

Chapter Eight

A Thought From Rescuing The Kitten

I pray Lord, by using this simple story, to show others of your Love – that they might recognize you as their Lord and Savior. Just as I am willing to come to the Light, I pray others will come to the Light and trust in you. In Christ's name, Amen!

We've got a kitten – very cute and playful. He has become the center of our attention from day one, and yes, the cat is spoiled-rotten. My 4-year-old son loves the cat very much. But he does not know how to treat a cat carefully. And so, my story begins:

One hot Monday afternoon, after we had been to the zoo, and enjoyed seeing all the animals, I was tired. I was playing the piano to relax, while my son was watching Curious George on TV. I heard the kitten meowing in a loud, loud voice, but I could not find him. The sound of the kitten was like he was in trouble, and terrified, but I could not see him anywhere. I began to worry.

I asked Josiah, "Where is the kitten?" He pointed to the refrigerator and said. "In there." I opened the door: The kitten was sitting on the shelf, screaming at the top of his lungs. I took out the shaking kitty and noticed his front paw was bleeding. I carried him to the bathroom, set him on the counter, and washed blood off of his chin, and tried to stop his paw from bleeding. I loved the kitten and talked to him, telling him he would be o-kay, and that he was such a good boy. Then I looked down and met my kittens eyes. I saw the expression of fear. As I loved him and petted him, the bleeding stopped. I could see from his eyes as he relaxed, and began to purr. The purring was like music to my ears, which relaxed me too.

I let the kitty loose, and as we sat down on the floor, I watched him dry himself. After awhile, as I was ready to get up, the cat ran towards me, rubbed himself against me, and purred loudly. I was glad to see him happy again. I held him, and we rubbed noses. The kitty would not leave me alone. He was so grateful and showed me all the love and appreciation a cat could think of for being rescued from that cold, dark frig. In his eyes, I was a hero, saving him from danger.

So from this story, may I illustrate the kitten's love to me as our love to God. We are sinners – lost in the dark – hopeless and helpless. But Christ came and retrieved us from sin, and set us free. He loved us with "His Everlasting Love," and He gave us assurance with His Word.

For it is written: **"Because he loves me," says the LORD, "I will rescue him; I will protect him, for he acknowledges my name"** (Psalm 91:14 NIV).

Thank you Lord for coming to my rescue. I am now safe and free in your Presence. **"The LORD is my light**

and my salvation; whom shall I fear? the LORD is the strength of my life" (Psalm 27:1). My kitten showed his love and appreciation to me by rubbing himself against me and purring loudly. As for me, I will praise you loudly and worship you with all my might. I show my love by following you and doing your will. I share my testimony with others, and tell the world about you (Matthew 28:19,20). Thank you LORD! I give you praise and glory, Amen!

Tuesday, April 27, 2010   11:44:54 AM

Written by Lei D. Cantrell

Chapter Nine

Return To The Master's House

We have a new addition in the house, a long-haired female chihuahua to accompany our two indoor cats. Her name is Cocoa, because she is a chocolate-brown color. And your heart will melt instantly when she looks at you with her two beautiful brown eyes.

She is also getting along very well with our two big outdoor dogs, at least as long as they obey her.

One night, when my husband came to pick me up from work, Cocoa was in the car and she was shaking. I thought she was cold, so I wrapped my coat around her. My husband explained that Cocoa had squeezed through the fence and was running loose on the street. Around midnight, everywhere was dark. I can imagine she was quite frightened, so when she saw my husband, she ran to him and sought his protection and love. She was so happy to be home.

From this simple story, may I direct your attention to Jesus' parable of how we are as sheep having gone astray, but when the shepherd calls his sheep, they know his voice, and follow him. (John 10:1-6).

Because "God is love" (1John 4:16), He is giving all of us opportunities to experience this Love. The yearning of our Father's heart is shown as He disciplines His children (Hebrew 12:5-11). He wants what is best for us because He cares deeply for us (1 Peter 5:7). He is very firm in His dealing with humanity. He sets people on a path to follow Him. He instructs those who come to know Him through His Son Jesus Christ (The Word) and His Holy Spirit. For those who do wrong, He chastens, He corrects. He becomes firm in order for us to realize His Sovereignty, His Lordship. His firmness is not to frighten us, but rather for us to change in our belief and behavior, and in our spirit, in order for us to grow to be more like Him – to be reconciled unto Him and His righteousness (2 Corinthians 5:20,21), and to become closer, more intimate with Him.

Because there are so many misconceptions of God's character in today's world, people tend to put God in the background or ignore him altogether. They think they can outsmart God, and do things their own way. So when people have fallen far far away from their Creator, they shut the door in God's face. It is only when they desperately need help, that they remember to call on Him. They expect Him to be like a Genie, to solve their problems quickly, but ignore Him again until the next time. So when circumstances worsen, and He has not answered their requests, that's when they doubt His existence, some to the point where they totally reject Him.

Please know that God is not someone that you can mold with your imagination. **"you thought I was altogether like you. But I will rebuke you . . . Consider this, you who forget God"** (Psalm 50:22,23 NIV). He is our Creator who deserves to be praised and worshipped with the uttermost respect and reverence. The fellowship between God and men must be renewed and refreshed constantly. If we are not in constant fellowship with Him, it is as if we are living without Him. In total rejection of God, we become empty, bitter, with broken hearts and despair through our entire being. It is only when we open our hearts again, to welcome Him back, that the Spirit of the Lord will help us to return and renew our fellowship with Him.

So, I pray that the Lord will guard our spirit and soul. When our spirit is down, we become so weak and easily tempted by this world. But we must remember it was Christ who died for our sin, that we have been purified by His shed blood. Therefore, we must look to the Lord, and return to our Master's house. **"For ye were as sheep going astray; but are now returned unto the Shepherd and Bishop of your souls"** (1 Peter 2:25).

Thank you Father for sending Jesus to die on the cross for our iniquity, so that we may have eternal life with you. Help us to follow your voice, and return to your house. In Jesus' name, Amen!

Saturday, September 20, 2014   12:38:54 AM

Written by Lei D. Cantrell

Chapter Ten

"Trust in Him at all times"
(Psalm 62:8)

Guess what? My house is full: I have five dogs (two outside) and two cats, plus two children, my husband and me! You must wonder where am I going with this? I will illustrate with a story and give the spiritual application.

One day last year, we let our indoor dog Cocoa out to potty, but instead of coming back in the house right away, she went to visit her friend in the neighborhood. She became pregnant with what turned out to be ten puppies. We were astonished! My daughter and I assisted during the delivery. One puppy didn't make it. Since Cocoa is an older(?) and small dog, she didn't have enough milk for all nine screaming pups. So we hand-fed the babies with puppy formula, and began to get attached to them. The puppies grew and grew and they were such joy to watch. By then it was so hard for us to give them away to good homes, but we kept two.

Remi and Angel are sweet most of the time. They love the cats, and will not leave them alone: Patches loves to play with them; Tiger not so much.

Each time I come home from work, both puppies would greet me at the door. Remi would stand up, and want to be held. And then he would want to play fetch.

One day, Remi was sick – his tummy was upset. He was feeling terrible. I got down on my knee, rubbed his tummy, and talked to him. He crawled under me and laid down for some more loving. I looked in his eyes and saw trust: He trusted me to make him feel better. Soon enough, he was himself again. He would run around the house and stop in front of me and would look up at me with gratitude in those big brown eyes. So whenever he feels bad, he would come lay down next to me. He knows that I would be there to comfort him.

Does that sound close-to-home? We can all be low-spirited sometimes: We all need comfort and assurance. And the only place for us to receive that is the Word of God. I like how Psalm 62:8 states, **"Trust in Him at all times; ye people, pour out your heart before Him: God is a refuge for us. Selah."**

I praise the Lord, for He is my **"refuge and strength, a very present help in trouble"** (Psalm 46:1). In Him alone I trust. Amen!

Saturday, September 13, 2014   2:44:27 PM

Written by Lei D. Cantrell

Chapter Eleven

My Savior's Love

The purpose of this story is to show that in the chaos of life, no matter how the world tries to get you down, Christ's love always comes through. So I praise the Lord for His Everlasting Love, which carried me through the chaos, and showed me that He is the Victory over all things. **"These things I have spoken unto you, that in me ye might have peace. In the world ye shall have tribulation: but be of good cheer; I have overcome the world"** (John 16:33). And He sends special people into my life to encourage me. His Love and "mercy endures forever."

It all goes back to one phone call I made to my mother, who told me that my dad was not doing well with his diabetes. Therefore, I should come visit or I'd regret that I didn't. So I started my international travel plan for the first time since being 20 years in the United States.

Both of my children wanted to go with me, since they had never been to China. So we applied for both kids' passports. An appointment for interview was made for Thursday, April 16th. At first, the main post office was totally booked, and there were not any openings until the end of April. Then there was a cancellation, so they squeezed us in. Praise the Lord. We went in and waited. When it was finally our turn, the lady took my daughter's picture first, and submitted her application. When it was my son's turn, he could not get a proper picture, because he has a condition called "Droopy Eye." He could not lift his eye lids and the strong light bothers him. When the lady behind the counter told him to look up to take his picture, he struggled but could not open his eyes wide enough. The lady said, "Well, this may spoil your trip. You have to write a letter with the doctor's note, then we will see what happens."

The Lord is so good and He alone knows the future. It just happened, our son Josiah had seen the eye specialist in March and the doctor had written a three page report on his condition. So when the lady asked for the doctor's report, we thanked the Lord that the report had come in handy. So on Friday April 17th, my husband wrote a letter and sent it in along with the doctor's report. We prayed for the application to go through. May God's name be praised – Josiah's passport came first in the mail just a week and a half after it was submitted; Our daughter's came three days later. I got so excited, I believe the Lord knew my anxious heart, that they approved my son's passport first in answer to my prayers.

Then came the month of May. I realized that my passport had been expired for 11 years. Since I have the green card as my identification, I didn't think about renewing my passport. Now that I was going back to visit,

I had to go to the Chinese Embassy in Chicago to renew my passport. So in the middle of May, Tim and I went to Chicago. After long hours of driving, including several hours of traffic jams, we arrived at the Embassy. It was a cold rainy Friday. I stood in front of Window 4, which is for serving Chinese citizens only. I was told to strictly speak in Chinese with the lady. She questioned and questioned. I answered and proved myself with everything she asked for. And after 2 hours, she said she would process the new passport, and was to mail it to us with the FedEx envelope we had provided for her.

We came home on Friday night. I had believed that everything went well at the Embassy. Then I received a phone call Monday afternoon from the lady, stating that she forgot to have me do electronic signing, and she wanted me to return to the Embassy. Otherwise, I would not get my passport. No way! I wanted to scream! Meanwhile, I received news from my mother, that my dad had gone into the hospital. His lungs and heart were filled with fluid and his legs were swollen. His kidneys were not functioning. He has been diabetic for over 30 years. I faxed the necessary paperwork to the lady at the Embassy. Then we waited. We had ordered the plane tickets for Saturday, June 14th. By the grace of God, I received my renewed passport. I praise the Lord for having everything in time for our departure.

While I was under such stress, I had several customers who comforted, encouraged, and prayed for me. I want to give special thanks to my dear friend Steven Lilley. Steve is among my regular customers who dine at Ryan's. What caught my attention was his gray hair – I should say that he has super blond hair that looks gray. He can cheer you up right away with his big smile. He is such a good listener: As I complained and whined about all of my troubles, he always replied with the biggest smile: "Don't worry Lei, give it all to God. He will make everything right for you." I honor and thank him for his encouragement and friendship. May God bless him richly.

The children and I did leave Saturday, June 14th, and arrived in Beijing, China on Monday, the16th. It was a long flight with turbulence along the way. We stayed with my parents for 3 weeks. My dad was able to get out of the hospital after being there for a month. It was a great reunion.

I thank the Lord for the blessings He has given, and I also thank the Lord for troubles as well. Although it seemed like it would never end at the time, God gave the victory, and He uses special people like Steve to be part of His plan to draw me closer to Him, and to know His Love through His Providence. How amazing! To God be the Glory, Amen!

Thursday, September 25, 2014   03:19:26 PM

Written by Lei D. Cantrell

Chapter Twelve

"I Surrender All"

I have resumed my life in Springfield, since returning from China in mid-July. I believed everyone back in China was basically doing well. My dad is stubborn and refuses dialysis, but he is stable, for which I am thankful.

Then I heard the bad news. It just happened that I sent a picture to my mom on the phone and asked how she liked my new dress. My brother answered instead, "Mom liked your dress, but she can't talk to you now. She has just come out of the surgery: They removed a tumor from her upper left lung." That really shocked me! I phoned my dad. He told me that they didn't want to worry me, so they didn't tell me. I found myself worried and frustrated. I went to work, but could not concentrate.

However, I thank the Lord for an encouraging word in the middle of the chaos. Ms. Jen is my manager. She is a small, but strong woman. She came to see me in the bakery while I was emotionally distressed. She spoke with such powerful words: "Lei, we are sorry to hear about your mother, and knowing that you can't be there with her right now. I know you believe in Jesus. Be strong in Jesus, believe God will take care of your mother. Give it all to Jesus!" With all my respect, what she said strengthened me.

The following week did not go well. My daughter got hit in the head with a softball while they were playing in a tournament, and was diagnosed with a minor concussion. She was having headaches, dizziness, nausea, pressure behind her left eye, and could not focus. The doctor recommended no sports whatsoever until she fully recovers.

Then my brother told me that mom's biopsy result shows the tumor is cancerous, however is not as serious. The CT scan shows there are small tumors growing in her right lung. They are going to treat her with traditional Chinese medicine. In three months, they will see if the tumors shrink. If not, they may decide to do surgery on the right lung.

There is an old saying, "When it rains, it pours." This certainly seemed to happen in my case. I found myself spiritually, emotionally, physically, and mentally drained. The pressure totally drove me to my knees. And as I was asking God to show me what to do, the song "I Surrender All" started ringing in my spirit:

"All to Jesus I surrender;
All to Him I freely give.
I will ever love and trust Him,
In His presence daily live.
All to Jesus I surrender;
Humbly at His feet I bow.

Worldly pleasures all forsaken,
Take me, Jesus, take me now.
I surrender all, I surrender all. . . ."

I believe God is showing me to surrender my burdens to Him. He knows that I cannot handle them in my own strength. He wants me to completely rest in His power. I thank you Lord for each reminder. May God's name be glorified through this trial. Amen!

Wednesday, February 15, 2017   01:31:55 AM

Written by Lei D. Cantrell

Chapter Thirteen

Jesus: The Perfect Example

The Holy Spirit inspired me to write on this subject. I pray that He will help us to follow Christ's example and better understand our Father's Heart. In Jesus name, Amen!

I have been troubled by world events lately. We are living in the end time (1 John 2:18). Studying bible prophecy only makes me wonder even more where we are on God's time table. There have been many false predictions that Christ would return at a certain time. Yet Jesus stated in Matthew 24:36, **"But of that day and hour knoweth no man, no, not the angels of heaven, but my Father only."**

I shared my thoughts with a few of my friends. Pastor Bob Nickel's response was rather striking: "Jesus is even now in submission to the Father in all things. Jesus says he is seated with the Father on his throne, not his own. 1 Corinthian 15 tells us that when Jesus has delivered up the earthly kingdom to the Father, he himself will continue to be in subjection to the Father for all eternity. He will always be visible to us as God manifested in the flesh! Jesus is fully God, yet he forever shows us the beauty of submission, so even as it relates to His coming for us, he voluntarily surrenders all of that to the Father. Jesus as the God–Man willingly accepts these limitations so He may more fully identify with us, and teach us submission, surrender, and trust in the Father's Sovereignty in all things."

How true! Indeed Jesus has been teaching us submission, surrender, and trust. When Jesus was tempted in the wilderness (Luke 4:2-13), in order to restore what Adam and Eve had lost, and overcome the world, Jesus passed the trial of temptation with confidence in God and God's Word without wavering.

Do you remember the Garden of Gethsemane? When he prayed: **"Father, if thou be willing, remove this cup from me: nevertheless not my will, but thine, be done"** (Luke 22:42). **"And being in an agony he prayed more earnestly: and his sweat was as it were great drops of blood falling down to the ground"** (Luke 22:44). **"Though he were a Son, yet learned he obedience by the things which he suffered"** (Heb. 5:8).

The Lord Jesus knows the Father's heart and purpose, thus he submitted himself to the Will of the Father. In order to restore the relationship between God and men, He surrendered and trusted Himself to God's Sovereignty.

So what is on the Father's heart? He is communicating through Jesus to us that He Loves us. He says, **"For God so loved the world, that He gave His only begotten Son, that whosoever believeth in him should not perish, but have everlasting life"** (John 3:16).

He desires to bless us: **"Delight thyself also in the LORD; and he shall give thee the desires of thine heart.**

Commit thy way unto the LORD; trust also in him; and he shall bring it to pass" (Psalm 37:4,5).

"Trust in him at all times; ye people, pour out your heart before him: God is a refuge for us. Selah" (Psalm 62:8).

It is never easy to submit, surrender, and trust. We often go for what is easy, comfortable, and convenient to suit our desires, but the result is not what we want it to be. But God does not change. He is all-powerful, He is always with us, He knows everything and sees everything. He even knows the future: He knows what He is doing! By faith, and daily fellowship with Him, we grow. And He, through His Spirit, reveals more of Himself to us: "Now we have received . . . the spirit which is of God; that we might know the things that are freely given to us of God" (1 Corinthians 2:12). When we call on the name of the Lord in times of trial, He delivers us, which increases our trust in Him. We need to learn to acknowledge Him in every aspect of our lives.

So we see that Jesus is our example, the perfect Son of God who submitting Himself to the Will of God The Father, suffered and died on the cross for the whole of humanity. He was resurrected on the third day, and is now seated at the right hand of God the Father. Praise God! How much more should we as the children of God follow Jesus' example and surrender ourselves to the Father.

"He that spared not his own Son, but delivered him up for us all, how shall he not with him also freely give us all things?" (Romans 8:32).

Lord, help us to know your heart. Help us to submit to your Will. Help us to surrender ourselves to you: Help us to trust you completely. Thank you Father for giving us examples to teach us, and to show your love for us. In Jesus' name, Amen!

Wednesday, October 01, 2014   10:50:32 PM

Written by Lei D. Cantrell

Chapter Fourteen

"Free, I am Free"

This chapter is in memory of a wonderful lady, Margaret Chow.

I have often heard questions asked in either Sunday School or bible study such as: "Does serving the Lord make us as slaves to God? What is the difference between slaves and servants?"

I would say the difference between slaves and servants is that slaves are enslaved forever. They can never be free, neither have they any joy: They have no hope. Servants have the opportunity to become free members of society upon completion of their service. As Christians, we are servants of God in a spiritual sense. When we are serving each other, we are doing so as unto God. We begin to experience true freedom the moment we receive salvation from God. And as we serve Him with all of our heart, mind, and spirit, we receive our reward when we complete our task. He will receive us and free us from all earthly bonds into the Heavenly Realm. And that's the most joyous occassion. I am sharing this testimony to support these thoughts.

My late friend Margaret Chow was half-British and half-Chinese. She was a missionary to South America. I first met her when I came to Springfield, MO. in 1993. Dr. June Kean, my sponsor, took me to Margaret's house to meet her. Dr. Kean thought that since Margaret was half-Chinese, we would have some things in common, and I wouldn't get as lonely, being so far away from home.

Margaret was a funny person. Sometimes, she would take me to Hong Kong Inn Chinese restuarant to eat, not far from Evangel College. She would open the fortune cookies and read the piece of paper. Then she would laugh and say, "My God holds my future, why would I listen to what this little piece of paper says?" As I was growing in the Lord, I found her way of witnessing quite comforting.

I stayed with her during holidays. I soon discovered Margaret was very passionate about God and His work. When there was a prayer meeting or bible study somewhere, nothing in this world could hinder her from participating. Watching her enthusiasm for the Lord caused me to want to be like her, and encouraged me to desire to know more of Christ. I praise the Lord for her.

Margaret began developing dementia about 3 years before passing away in March of 2014. She was 97 years young. According to her daughter, she went to get her hair done the day before her passing. Then she went to meet her Maker.

I went to her graveside service and listened to the testimonies of how Margaret had touched peoples' lives. I was glad that I was one of them.

As I was thinking about Margaret, how Heaven was rejoicing over her Homecoming, and how much I will miss her, I felt sad. The Lord knew my heart, so He showed me a vision while I slept. In the vision, I was sitting in a huge auditorium. I saw a lot of people standing on the platform. Margaret was being introduced to all the people. She looked as beautiful as ever. When being asked to speak to the audience, she looked at everyone with a big smile and said, "Free, I am Free." The entire place cheered, and the angels started rejoicing. I awoke from my sleep, and felt peace. I thanked the Lord for the precious vision I was given.

This world is full of sin. Because we are Christians, we are to share the good news, even though we often receive rejection. And as we are human, we are to endure the pain of our flesh. From that vision, I have come to a new understanding of Heaven: It is Freedom from physical, emotional, and spiritual battles as well.

> **"For the Lamb which is in the midst of the throne shall feed them, and shall lead them unto living fountains of waters: and God shall wipe away all tears from their eyes"** (Revelation 7:17).

> **"And God shall wipe away all tears from their eyes; and there shall be no more**

**death, neither sorrow, nor crying, neither
shall there be any more pain; for the former
things are passed away"** (Revelation 21:4).

Amen! Shout and give Glory to God the Most High.
We will be free, and free indeed when we are fully in His
Presence. How marvelous it will be when that Day comes. I
praise the Lord for this vision. Margaret is indeed free, and
rejoicing in the Heavenly Realm. I will join her someday.
Praise the Lamb of God, Amen!

Thursday, February 11, 2016   01:44:50 AM

Written by Lei D. Cantrell

Chapter Fifteen

God Hears

As we live our daily lives, we are busy with our families, work, friends, etc. We may easily get side-tracked by all of the earthly things. Sometimes we pray, and then move on to the next thing. How often do we wonder if God has heard our prayer. Does He answer our prayers in due time, whether we realize it or not?

I find it amazing how the Scriptures record that God Listens:

In Psalm 4:3 it says, "But know that the Lord hath set apart him that is godly for himself: the Lord will hear when I call unto him."

Psalm 34:4 states: "I sought the Lord, and he heard me, and delivered me from all my fears."

Psalm 66:19 says, "But verily God hath heard me; he hath attended to the voice of my prayer."

"In my distress I called upon the LORD, and cried unto my God: he heard my voice out of his temple, and my cry came before him, even into his ears" (Psalm 18:6).

"I love the LORD, because he hath heard my voice and my supplications" (Psalm 116:1).

"I will praise thee: for thou hast heard me, and art become my salvation" (Psalm 118:21).

"In my distress I cried unto the LORD, and He heard me" (Psalm 120:1).

And there are many more. God listens.

Okay, it is true that God listens to us – His children's cries, pleas, complaints, heartfelt prayers. How does our Father respond?

Please allow me to use the terror attack on Paris as an example. The incident drew worldwide attention. Then the Syrian refugees poured into this country, and possible terrorists were among them. The Missouri Governor's response was rather chilling. In my mind, I struggled with thoughts of how safe is my family, and how will I go to work and leave my child at school? All of those thoughts got me so upset and nervous.

So one morning, while I was at work, my mind could not stop having those fears. Suddenly, the Spirit of the Lord spoke to my spirit: "Stop that! Your job is to feed my people, and I will do the rest!" I was literally struck by the Word of the Lord. The fear – all the struggle I had – left me instantly: The joy of the Lord came within me instead.

I am sure everyone has their own struggles in life. But the truth is that God is here and listens, and He would not allow us to go through the tough times without coming to rescue us according to His Word.

When we are down, we tend to struggle with our feelings, and get nowhere. It is true God is here to listen, but we must surrender to Him. 1 Peter 5:7 says so well, **"Casting all your care upon Him, for he careth for you."**

Now I will praise the Lord for His goodness toward His children. **"O Praise the LORD, all ye nations: praise him, all ye people. For his merciful kindness is great toward us: and the truth of the LORD endureth for ever. Praise ye the LORD"** (Psalm 117:1,2).

Wednesday, June 08, 2016   05:41:20 PM

Written by Lei D. Cantrell

Chapter Sixteen

How Eager Are You For The Strength Of The Lord?

**"The LORD will give strength unto his people;
the LORD will bless his people
with peace" (Psalm 29:11).**

Father, I thank you for your Word, which has been my strength. I pray you use this testimony to encourage each one to seek you for strength and comfort. May your Word help us to look to you for guidance. May your Word strengthen us as we go about our daily routines. In Jesus name I pray, Amen!

Have you had any days when you wake up in the morning and you don't feel like doing anything? You just want to go back to sleep! When you drag your tired body to work and wish this day to be quickly over? For the sake of paying the bills, you have to stay there, and the whole day feels like eternity. When you are having one of those days, what do you do?

I have had a few of those days. I rarely drink coffee, but to keep me awake and to be energized, I do. Since I am not a regular coffee drinker, my eyes open up extremely big after the third sip, and as soon as I finish the half cup of coffee, I can feel the effect of caffeine like a motor turning on in my body. Like the Energizer Bunny, I keep going, and going and going. That has been exactly how I felt: It kept me going until the end of my shift.

When we are weak and weary, sometimes we go after the things in this world to help us. The caffeine can only take effect on me for a few hours, then it will totally wear out.

Now can we look at what the Word of God says? **Psalm 73:26 (NIV) tells us: "My flesh and my heart may fail, but God is the strength of my heart and my portion forever." Isaiah 40:29 declares: "He giveth power to the faint; and to them that have no might he increaseth strength."** The caffeine effect is temporary, but the Word of God is eternal. The scripture perfectly portrays this truth: **"And be not conformed to this world, but be ye transformed by the renewing of your mind, that you may prove what is that good, and acceptable, and perfect will of God" (Romans 12:2).**

How shall we draw strength from the Lord? I praise Him, for He is my strength: **"Behold, God is my salvation; I will trust, and not be afraid: for the LORD YAHWEH is my strength and my song; he also is become my salvation." (Isaiah 12:2).**

Now as you are running out of the temporary strength from this world, my question is: How eagerly are you seeking the Strength of the Lord?

Tuesday, February 20th, 2018.   2:10pm

Written by Lei Deng Cantrell

Chapter Seventeen

"I Know Who You Are"

God is Personal. Many people today think of God as an unseen Spiritual Being, sitting up there far away in some heavenly realm – irrelevant! Or they believe that God is too busy running the Universe to have time for individuals. I disagree with both. Let me explain:

Since He created everything (Ephesians 3:9), including each one of us, for a purpose (2 Timothy 1:9), He is personally involved. As a matter of fact, He holds everything together (Colossians 1:17). Since He made us and knows who we are – our character, personality, and desires – He works our lives toward an eternal fulfillment, according to whether we choose to submit and honor Him or go our own way.

I went to work one day without my name tag. When I told my boss, his calm response was, "I know who you are!" The rest of the day, I did my job without worrying what anyone else thought. At Chick-Fil-A, where I now work, we are always reminded by the owners that we are there to serve the Lord.

Have you ever been accused of something that you did not do? Recently, I was accused of wrongdoing by a customer. My supervisor came and asked me about it. I was innocent, but I was upset over the customers accusation. My supervisor said, "I know you, and I believe that you did not say such a thing. So everything is well."

I was grateful for her trust and confidence in me, but my heart was troubled, and I did not want to go to work the next day. As I was dragging myself to get dressed, the Spirit of God spoke to my spirit: "Do not let your heart be troubled, neither be dismayed." Wow, can you imagine what these words did for me? I was immediately encouraged. The dread left me, and the joy of the Lord came in. I went to work in a good spirit and served the customers as the Lord intended.

Often we are troubled by the world, and we forget our identity as followers of Christ. That is when we may act worldly. But God uses people and circumstances to strengthen us, and to remind us of His Presence. **"And the peace of God, which passeth all understanding, shall keep your hearts and minds through Christ Jesus"** (Philippians 4:7).

Finally, I remind you of this: The Lord says, "I know who you are!" Now it is your responsibility to follow Him. It is never too late to find out your citizenship is in Heaven. It is never too soon to seek a closer relationship with your Heavenly Father. Christ said in John 8:12, **"I am the Light of the world. Whoever follows me will never walk in darkness, but will have the light of Life (NIV)."** I pray that you will accept Him as your Lord and Savior, and have Him become the center of your life. Amen!

Friday, February 07, 2014   9:47:38 AM

Written by Lei D. Cantrell

My Final Thoughts

"God is love." However, there are so many circumstances in the world which cause people not to feel or sense His Presence. Because I understand how you feel, I am sharing my recent Bible study to show how much He loves us.

The Deep Love of God

God is Gracious – meaning merciful, compassionate, kind, forgiving, forbearing, tenderhearted, sympathetic, generous, benevolent.

But how do we understand His Grace? He shows Grace to humanity by sending His beloved Son to reverse what Adam and Eve had lost. He desires for us to receive this free Gift in order to return to Him.

Jesus Himself fulfilled the commandments of the Father:

1. He set an example of passing tests of temptation without wavering

2. Being baptized as a symbol of death, burial and resurrection.
3. He taught the knowledge of God.
4. He was sacrificed on the cross as a Ransom for all.
5. He was resurrected by the Father on the third day. The whole process was a full accomplishment of God's Will.

I do not have the words to describe my gratitude for what He has done.

We can see how God shows His love to us:

A. "Love is kind, it suffers (endures) long, it never fails" (1 Cor. 13: 4,7,8).

1. He gives us Christ – to die on the cross for our transgressions.
2. He gives us His Word – to instruct us.
3. He gives us His Holy Spirit – to lead us, and to comfort us.

B. "Love is Patient" – how patient is our God?

1. He suffers with us when we suffer (Philippians 1:29).
2. He is always there to pick us up, to strengthen, to encourage, to discipline (Psalm 138:3,7), (Revelation 3:19).
3. He patiently waits if we go astray. We can see the example of Jesus' parable of the lost son (Luke 15:11-24).

C. He calls His people to Him, to draw them close: **"I have loved you with an everlasting love: therefore with lovingkindness have I drawn thee"** (Jeremiah 31:3).

So what is our reward for receiving the Love of God? We are washed clean, to be able to spend eternity with Him. **"And this is the record, that God hath given to us eternal life, and this life is in his Son. He that hath the Son hath life; and he that hath not the Son of God hath not life"** (1 John 5:11,12). And while we are here, we have His hope, peace, and joy.

However, God's Love for us did not stop when Christ ascended back to the Father. This is why He sent His Spirit – The third person of the Holy Trinity – to be with us, so we can be led, comforted, and through Him we can enhance our walk with God.

Now that we have studied God's Grace and Love, do you know Him and His Love? Does your heart long for the Love of God? If you do, why not seek Him? For He has said: **"Ask, and it shall be given you; seek, and ye shall find; knock, and it shall be opened unto you"** (Matthew 7:7). Get to know Him, and you shall receive Hope, Joy and Peace. I pray you will find Him. Welcome Him into your life and let Him renew you. Let Him draw you close to Him, so that you may rejoice in His Presence.

I conclude with this poem as a prayer of devotion to Him:

Dear LORD,
Hear our praises, Lord.
It is You who created us,
We found peace and comfort in You.
We rejoice in You and praise You for Your work.
"In Him our hearts rejoice, for we
trust in His Holy Name"
(Psalm 33:21 NIV).
Our hearts trust in You, O Lord. For You are Mighty.
Our hearts long for Your Return.
Our Lord, we devote ourselves to You,
Let us behold You!
Let no one deny!
Our hearts cry out to You,
Only You can understand us,
Only You can comfort us,
In You we seek shelter.
You are our Light in the darkness,
You are our Guide to righteousness.
Strengthen us with your Word,
that we may rest in You.
We praise You Almighty God.
Thanks and Glory belong to You,

In Christ Jesus, we shall abide.
Amen!

About the Author

It has been twenty-five years since the Lord brought Lei Deng Cantrell from Beijing, China to Springfield, MO. so that she might know Him, follow Him, and learn to do His Will.

Her First book, One In A Billion, shares with the audience her testimony – how she came to know the Lord and what God has done in her first ten years of journey with Him.

Lei has been working in food service for over 20 years, sharing her testimony with co-workers and customers, to both neighbors and to people from all over the world, along with her church family at Southern Heights Bible Church.

Her new book – My Heart Longs For The Lord – invites the audience on a journey to see how God has been revealing Himself through the obstacles of this life to cause her to grow in and closer to Him.

Lei and her husband Tim have been married 21 years. They have two children, Leianna and Josiah. Both are growing in the Lord, and are such a blessing from the Lord.

Printed in the United States
By Bookmasters